Guess What!

Pupil's Book 4

British English

Susannah Reed with Kay Bentley

Series Editor: Lesley Koustaff

CAMBRIDGE
UNIVERSITY PRESS

Contents

Welcome back!

Guess What!

1 [CD1 02] **Listen and point.**

2 [CD1 03] **Listen, point and repeat.**

Tom

Lucas

Lily

Max

Anna

3 [CD1 04] **Listen and say the names.**

4 Think **Describe and guess who.**

Is it a girl or a boy?   It's a boy.

Has he got dark hair?   No, he hasn't.

Is it Tom?   Yes, it is.

❶ dark hair
❷ straight hair
❸ glasses
❹ fair hair
❺ curly hair
❻ red hair

→ Activity Book page 4

5 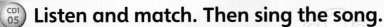 **CD1 05 Listen and match. Then sing the song.**

1 What does Fred look like?
He's tall, he's got blue eyes,
And he's got red hair.
He's got short red hair.

2 What does Jane look like?
She's tall, she's got brown eyes,
And she's got straight hair.
She's got long straight hair.

3 What does Paul look like?
He's short, he's got brown eyes,
And he's got dark hair.
He's got short dark hair.

6 Look at page 6. Read and match.

1 What does Lucas look like?

a She's tall. She's got long straight hair.

2 What does Lily look like?

b He's short. He's got brown eyes.

3 What does Tom's sister look like?

c He's tall. He's got short fair hair.

4 What does Anna's brother look like?

d She's short. She's got red hair.

7 (About Me) **Think about your family. Ask and answer.**

What does your cousin look like?

She's short and she's got straight dark hair.

Remember!

What does **he look like**?
He's tall.
He's got blue eyes.

→ Activity Book page 5

Grammar **7**

8 (CD1 06) **Listen and repeat.**

100 cm = 1 m

10 cm | 20 cm | 30 cm | 40 cm | 50 cm | 60 cm | 70 cm | 80 cm | 90 cm | 100 cm

9 (CD1 07) **Listen and match. Then ask and answer with a friend.**

a **76 cm**

b **1 m 32 cm**

c **91 cm**

d **1 m 67 cm**

e **1 m 19 cm**

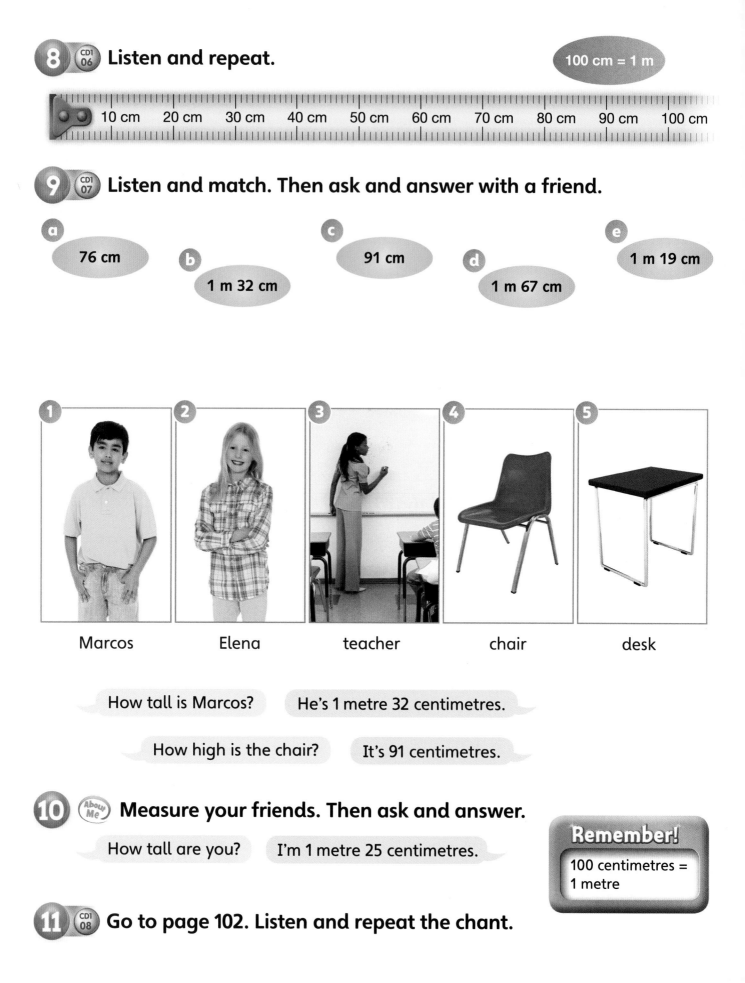

1 Marcos
2 Elena
3 teacher
4 chair
5 desk

How tall is Marcos?   He's 1 metre 32 centimetres.

How high is the chair?   It's 91 centimetres.

10 (About Me) **Measure your friends. Then ask and answer.**

How tall are you?   I'm 1 metre 25 centimetres.

Remember!
100 centimetres = 1 metre

11 (CD1 08) **Go to page 102. Listen and repeat the chant.**

→ Activity Book page 6

Skills: *Reading and speaking*

Let's start! **What activities do you do with your friends?**

12 CD1 09 **Read and listen. Then match.**

My friends

c

1 My best friend's name is Rosa. She's very tall. She's 1 metre 36 centimetres! She's got long dark hair and brown eyes. We like music and we like playing the recorder together. We have recorder lessons every Wednesday.

2 This is my friend Louis. He's got straight dark hair and green eyes. We're in the same class at school. We like playing table tennis. We play after school on Wednesdays. We like badminton too.

3 This is me with my friends Sally and James. We like horse riding. We have riding lessons on Sundays and we like looking after the horses too. Horses are my favourite animals. They're beautiful.

a

b

13 **Read again and answer the questions.**

1 How tall is Rosa?
2 Does Rosa have recorder lessons on Sundays?
3 What does Louis look like?
4 What day do Sally and James go horse riding?

14 About Me **Think of a friend and answer the questions.**

What's his or her name?
What does he or she look like?
Do you like the same things?
What activities do you do together?

Writing

→ Activity Book page 7: Write about a friend and what they like doing.

Value: Get involved with your local community → Activity Book page 8

16 CD1 11 Talk Time **Listen and repeat. Then act.**

watching TV   going ice skating   making models
playing the guitar   going bowling   playing table tennis

1 What shall we do today?
How about watching TV?
OK, then.

2 What shall we do today?
How about playing the guitar?
No, let's go fishing.
OK, good idea.

Say it!

17 CD1 12 **Listen and repeat.**

Owls make no sound when they fly down.

owl

What patterns can you see?

1 (CD1 13) **Listen and repeat.**

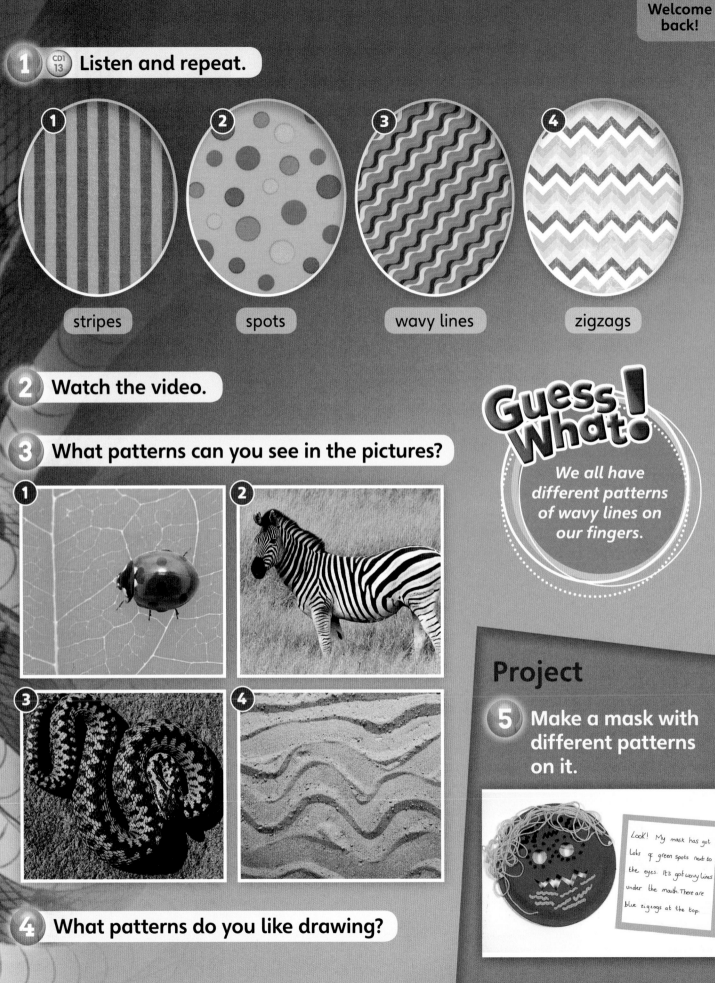

① stripes

② spots

③ wavy lines

④ zigzags

2 **Watch the video.**

3 **What patterns can you see in the pictures?**

Guess What!

We all have different patterns of wavy lines on our fingers.

Project

5 **Make a mask with different patterns on it.**

Look! My mask has got lots of green spots next to the eyes. It's got wavy lines under the mouth. There are blue zigzags at the top.

4 **What patterns do you like drawing?**

1 Fun sports

Guess What!

1 (CD1 14) **Listen and point.**

2 (CD1 15) **Listen, point and repeat.**

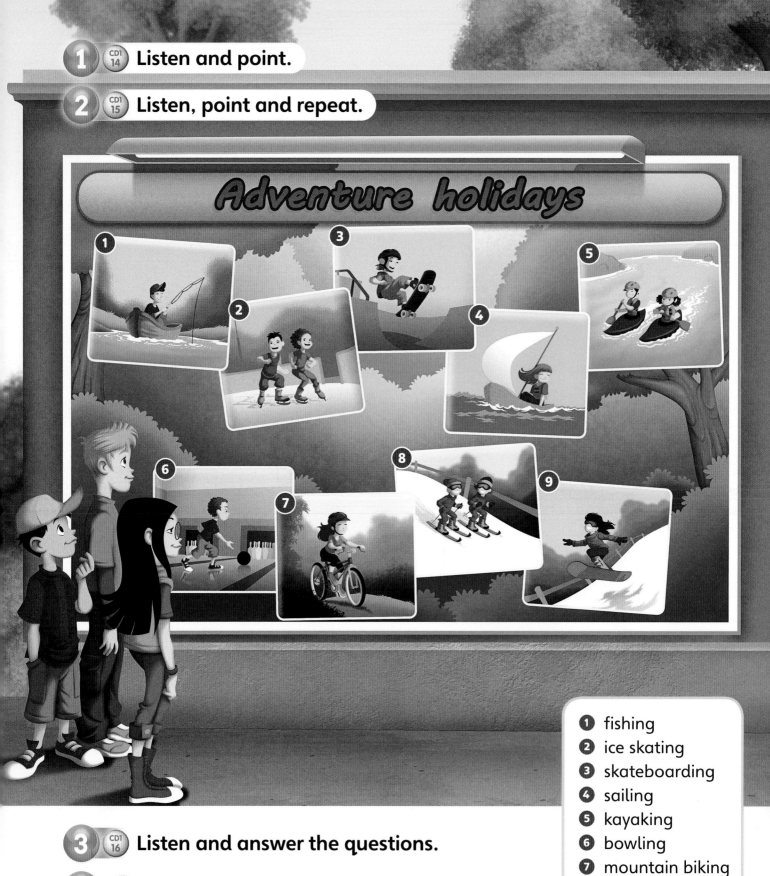

Adventure holidays

3 (CD1 16) **Listen and answer the questions.**

4 (About Me) **Ask and answer with a friend.**

Do you like skiing?   Yes, I do.

❶ fishing
❷ ice skating
❸ skateboarding
❹ sailing
❺ kayaking
❻ bowling
❼ mountain biking
❽ skiing
❾ snowboarding

→ Activity Book page 12

5 CD1 17 **Listen and choose. Then sing the song.**

1 I'm good at ice skating/mountain biking,
But I'm not very good at skiing.
Sally isn't good at ice skating/mountain biking,
But she's very good at skiing.
Sally is a good friend,
But we're good at different things.
Yes! Sally is a good friend,
But we're good at different things.

2 I'm good at snowboarding/skateboarding,
But I'm not very good at sailing.
Ricky isn't good at snowboarding/
skateboarding,
But he's very good at sailing.
Ricky is a good friend,
But we're good at different things.
Yes! Ricky is a good friend,
But we're good at different things.

6 About Me **Make sentences about you and your friends. Say *true* or *false*.**

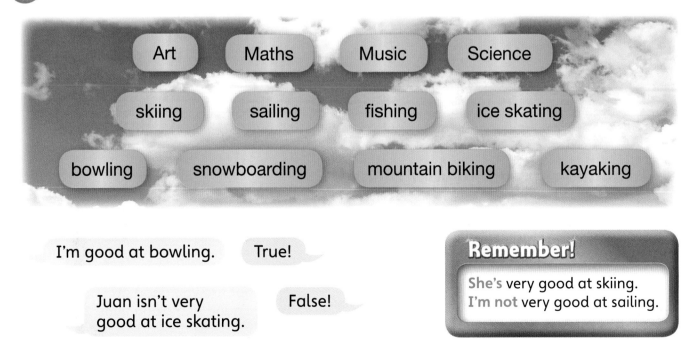

| Art | Maths | Music | Science |

| skiing | sailing | fishing | ice skating |

| bowling | snowboarding | mountain biking | kayaking |

I'm good at bowling.   True!

Juan isn't very good at ice skating.   False!

Remember!
She's very good at skiing.
I'm not very good at sailing.

→ Activity Book page 13

Grammar **17**

7 (CD1 18) **Listen and repeat.**

1 Are you good at skiing?

Yes, I am.

No, I'm not.

2 What are you good at?

I'm good at ice skating.

8 (Think) **Look and choose. Then ask and answer with a friend.**

1

2

3

4

5

6

7

8

9

9 **Tell the class about your friend.**

Matthew is good at playing table tennis.

10 (CD1 19) **Go to page 102. Listen and repeat the chant.**

Remember!

Are you good at playing the guitar?
Yes, I am.   No, I'm not.
What are you good at?
I'm good at making films.

Skills: *Listening and speaking*

Let's start! **Do you like talent shows?**

11 🎧CD1 20 **Listen and match.**

Forest School Talent Show!
4.30 this afternoon in the school hall.

1 Mel **2 Kim** **3 Alex**

a b c

12 🎧CD1 20 **Listen again and answer the questions.**

1 How old is Mel?
2 Is Kim good at making films?
3 Can Alex play the piano?
4 Who is the winner of the talent show?

13 About Me **Plan a talent show with your friends.**

What are you good at?

I'm good at music. I can play the piano.

I can sing!

Writing

→ Activity Book page 15: Plan a talent show.

15 CD2 22 Talk Time **Listen and repeat. Then act.**

> wash the car   paint a picture   make a film
> write a story   make a cake   sing a song

1

Who wants to make a cake?

I do. I'm good at making cakes.

2

Who wants to paint a picture?

I don't. I'm not good at Art.

Say it!

16 CD1 23 **Listen and repeat.**

Royal pythons coil into balls on the soil.

royal python

What type of
body movements
can we make?

1 CD1 24 **Listen and repeat.**

1 turn
2 shake
3 bend
4 stretch
5 kick

2 **Watch the video.**

3 **What body movements are the children making in these pictures?**

1
2
3
4

Guess What!

We all make the same body movement when we're happy. We smile.

Project

5 Write body movements for a street dance.

Movement	Number
Stretch arms and turn	1
kick	2
jump	4
Shake your body	4
kick	2
stretch arms and turn	1

4 **What body movements do you make in sport?**

→ Activity Book page 18

CLIL: Physical Education **23**

Guess What!

25

1 **CD1 25** Listen and point.

2 **CD1 26** Listen, point and repeat.

3 **CD1 27** Listen and say the words.

4 **Think** Look at Tom's map. Describe and guess where.

It's opposite the park.   Museum!

1. shopping centre
2. square
3. underground station
4. hotel
5. traffic light
6. museum
7. restaurant
8. bank
9. zebra crossing
10. bus station

5  **Listen and match. Then sing the song.**

1 Where's the museum?
It's in the square.
It's opposite the hotel.
Can you see it over there?

2 Where's the underground station?
It's below the square.
It's near the shopping centre.
Can you see it over there?

3 Where's the plane?
It's above the square.
It's far from the town.
Can you see it up there?

6 **Read and match.**

1 Where's the museum?

2 Where's the plane?

3 Where's the shopping centre?

4 Where's the underground station?

a It's near the underground station.

b It's below the square.

c It's above the square.

d It's opposite the hotel.

7 (About Me) **Make a map of your town. Then ask and answer.**

Where's the bank?

It's opposite the school.

No, it isn't! It's next to the museum!

Remember!

Where's the bus station?
It's **far from** the hotel.

8 (CD1 29) **Listen and repeat.**

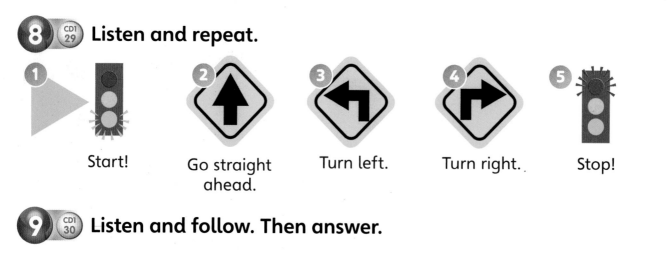

1 Start!

2 Go straight ahead.

3 Turn left.

4 Turn right.

5 Stop!

9 (CD1 30) **Listen and follow. Then answer.**

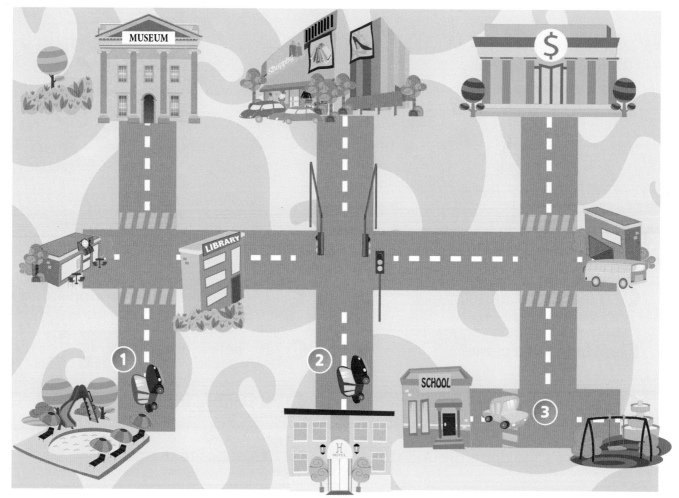

10 (Think) **Play the game with a friend.**

Start at the restaurant.   Go straight ahead.

Remember!
Start at the hotel. Turn right at the library.

11 (CD1 31) **Go to page 102. Listen and repeat the chant.**

Skills: *Reading and speaking*

Let's start! **What can you see in your town?**

12 (CD1 32) **Read and listen. Then match.**

My trip to London!

Morning [1] This is London Zoo. It's really big. It's near my hotel. There are lots of animals in the zoo. This is the giraffe house. Giraffes are my favourite animal.

Lunch [2] This is the Rainforest Café. It's my favourite restaurant in London. What can you see behind the tables? They're elephants!

Afternoon [3] This is the Science Museum. And this is my favourite room – the transportation area. There are lots of cars and a lorry. And look above the people. There's a plane!

Evening [4] This is Trafalgar Square. There's a big art gallery here. There are statues and a fountain, too.

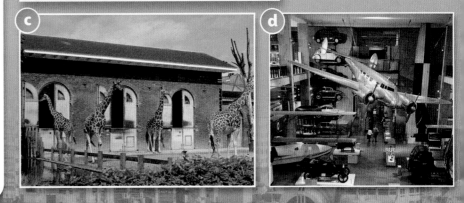

13 **Read again and choose the words.**

1 London Zoo is near/far from his hotel.
2 The Rainforest Café is his favourite shopping centre/restaurant.
3 There's a plane above/below the people in the Science Museum.
4 There's a big art gallery/bus station in Trafalgar Square.

14 (About Me) **Ask and answer with a friend.**

What's your favourite city?
What can you see there?

Writing

→ Activity Book page 23: Write about your favourite city.

15 CD1 33 **Read and listen.**

Value: Cycle safely

→ Activity Book page 24

16 CD1 34 Talk Time **Listen and repeat. Then act.**

library   sports field   shopping centre
supermarket   bus station   dining hall

1

Excuse me. How do you get to the **bus station**?

Turn left at the zebra crossing and go straight ahead.

Thank you.

2

Excuse me. How do you get to the **shopping centre**?

Turn right at the traffic lights and go straight ahead.

Thank you.

Say it!

17 CD1 35 **Listen and repeat.**

Turtles whirl in the surf.

→ Activity Book page 25   Function: Asking for directions   Pronunciation: *ur / ir*   **31**

What 3D shapes can you see?

1 [CD1 36] Listen and repeat.

| sphere | cylinder | cone | cube | pyramid |

2 Watch the video.

3 What shapes can you see? Read and match.

1 This building is a pyramid shape with glass squares.
2 This building is a cube shape.
3 This building has cylinders at the front.
4 This building is a cone shape.
5 This building has a glass sphere on top.

Guess What!

Some Mexican pyramids are 3,000 years old but some Egyptian pyramids are 4,000 years old.

4 What shapes can you see in buildings near your school?

Project

5 Make 3D paper buildings for a town.

In this town the buildings are different shapes. There are cylinders, cones, cubes and pyramids.

Review Units 1 and 2

1 Find the words in the puzzles and match to the photos.

fis	boarding
skate	hing
kaya	arding
snowbo	king

Fred

Alice

2 (CD1 37) Listen and say the names.

3 Answer the questions.

1 Where's Fred?
2 What's Josh good at?
3 Is Mia good at skiing?
4 Is Alice in the square?

4 Make your own word puzzles for your friend.

Choose activities
or places in town:
super   urant
resta   market

Josh

Mia

→ Activity Book pages 28–29

	A	B	C	D
1				
2				
3				
4				

Red
Are you good at (skateboarding)?

Blue
What does he/she look like?

Green
Where's the (bus station)?

Number 1. Letter A. — Are you good at skateboarding? — Yes, I am.

35

3 At work

Guess What!

1 CD1 38 **Listen and point.**

2 CD1 39 **Listen, point and repeat.**

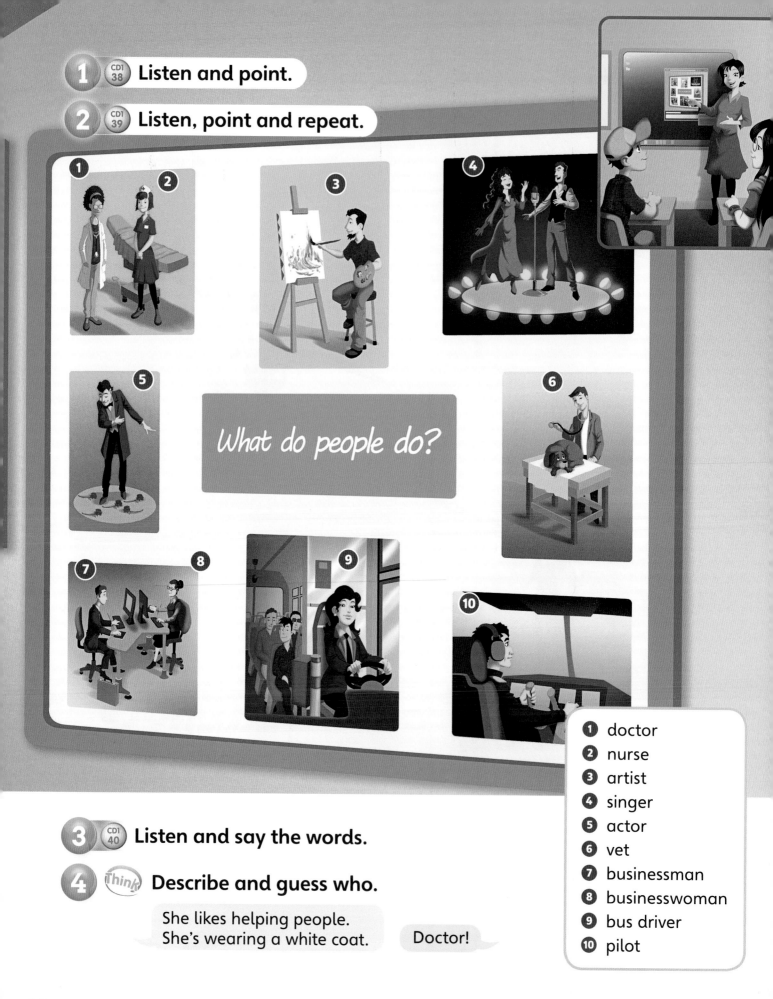

What do people do?

3 CD1 40 **Listen and say the words.**

4 Think **Describe and guess who.**

She likes helping people.
She's wearing a white coat.

Doctor!

1 doctor
2 nurse
3 artist
4 singer
5 actor
6 vet
7 businessman
8 businesswoman
9 bus driver
10 pilot

5 (CD1 41) **Listen and choose. Then sing the song.**

1 What does your aunt do? …
She's an artist/singer.
Where does she work? …
She works in a studio.

2 What does your uncle do? …
He's a bus driver/pilot.
Where does he work? …
He works on a plane.

3 What does your cousin do? …
She's a businesswoman/doctor.
Where does she work? …
She works in an office.

6 **Read and match.**

1 My dad's a farmer. He works on a farm.

2 My grandma's a teacher. She works in a school.

3 My mum's a train driver. She works on a train.

4 My grandpa's a doctor. He works in a hospital.

7 (About Me) **Think about your family.
Ask and answer.**

What does your cousin do?

He's a nurse.

Where does he work?

He works in a hospital.

Remember!

What does your aunt do?
She's an artist.
Where does she work?
She works in a studio.

→ Activity Book page 31

8 (CD1 42) **Listen and repeat.**

9 (About Me) **Choose what you want to be. Then ask and answer.**

10 **Tell the class about your friend.**

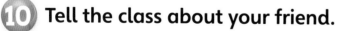

Sally wants to be an actor.

11 (CD1 43) **Go to page 102. Listen and repeat the chant.**

Remember!

What do you want to be?
I want to be a teacher.

Skills: *Listening and speaking*

Let's start! **Where do you want to work?**

12 (CD1 44) **Listen and match.**

Sanjay

a

b

Lola

c

d

13 (CD1 44) **Listen again and say *true* or *false*.**

1 Sanjay's good at Science.
2 Sanjay wants to be a doctor.
3 Lola wants to work in an office.
4 Lola's good at English.

14 (About Me) **Ask and answer with a friend.**

What are you good at?
Do you want to work with animals or people?
Do you want to work in a school or in an office?

Writing

→ Activity Book page 33: Write about what you want to be and where you want to work.

16 CD1 46 Talk Time **Listen and repeat. Then act.**

give some water to the horse   feed the rabbit   feed the cat
give some milk to the cat   take the dog for a walk

1

Shall I take the dog for a walk?

Yes, please.

2

Shall I feed the cat?

No, thanks, but you can feed the rabbit.

OK.

Say it!

17 CD1 47 **Listen and repeat.**

Crabs crawl across sand.

crab

What type of
work
is it?

1 **Listen and repeat.**

outdoor work

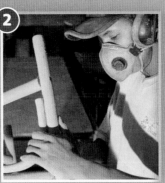
factory work

transport work

shop work

2 **Watch the video.**

3 **Look at the pictures. What type of work can you see?**

Guess What!

We know how old a tree is from the number of circles in its wood.

Project

5 *From trees to shops. Make a poster.*

4 **What types of work do you think are difficult?**

Wild animals

Guess What!

1 CD1 49 **Listen and point.**

2 CD1 50 **Listen, point and repeat.**

3 CD1 51 **Listen and say the animals.**

4 Think **Describe and guess what.**

It's brown and it can jump. It's got a long tail.

Kangaroo!

1 kangaroo
2 koala
3 parrot
4 penguin
5 bat
6 owl
7 jaguar
8 bear
9 panda
10 gorilla

5 🎵 52 Listen and match. Then sing the song.

1 Gorillas are bigger than pandas,
But gorillas are smaller than bears.
Bears are bigger than gorillas,
And they're bigger than pandas too.
Animals, animals. Look at the animals!

2 Bats are noisier than koalas,
But bats are quieter than parrots.
Parrots are noisier than bats,
And they're noisier than koalas too.
Animals, animals. Look at the animals!

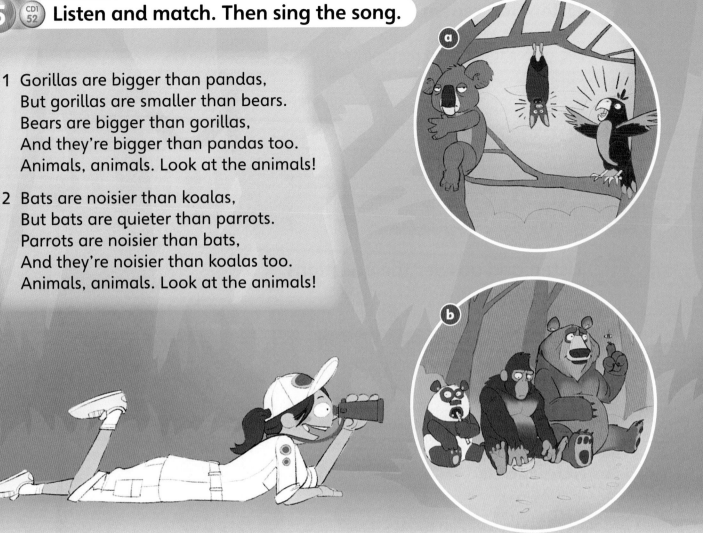

6 Read and say *true* or *false*.

1 Pandas are smaller than bears.
2 Gorillas are bigger than bears.
3 Bears are bigger than pandas.
4 Bats are noisier than parrots.
5 Koalas are quieter than bats.
6 Parrots are quieter than koalas.

7 About Me Make sentences about your favourite animals. Say *true* or *false*.

Tigers are quicker than rabbits.

True!

Remember!

big**ger**
small**er**
nois**ier**
quiet**er**

8 (CD1 53) **Listen and repeat.**

1 Are giraffes taller than penguins?

Yes, they are.

2 Are koalas noisier than bears?

No, they aren't.

9 (CD1 54) **Listen and answer the questions.**

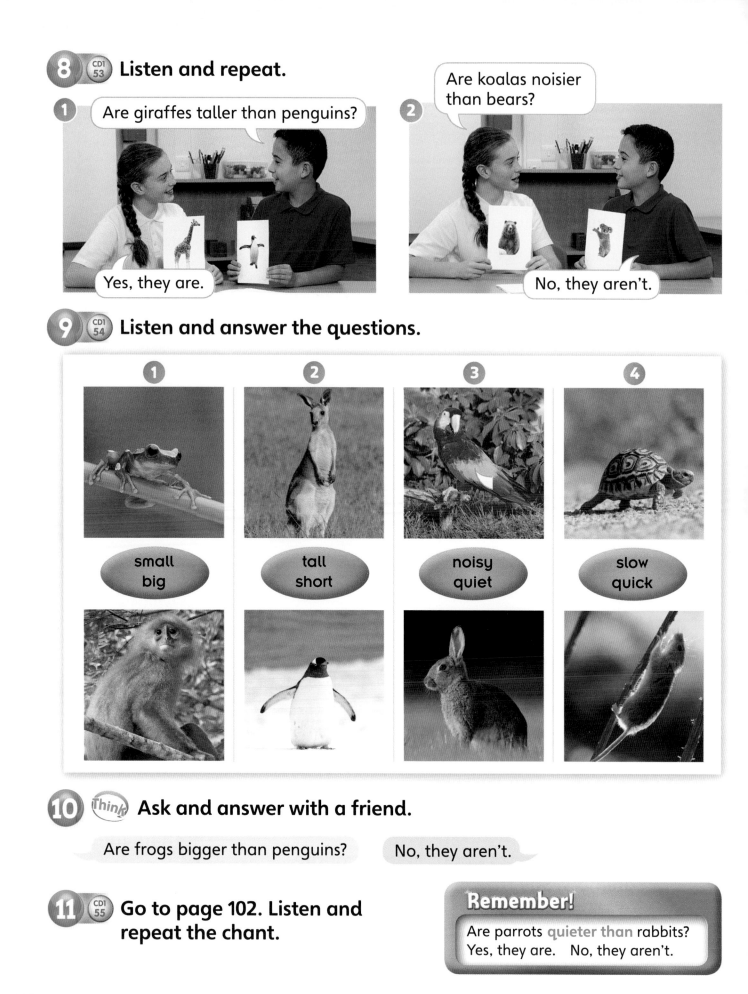

1 small / big

2 tall / short

3 noisy / quiet

4 slow / quick

10 (Think) **Ask and answer with a friend.**

Are frogs bigger than penguins?   No, they aren't.

11 (CD1 55) **Go to page 102. Listen and repeat the chant.**

Remember!

Are parrots quieter than rabbits?
Yes, they are.   No, they aren't.

→ Activity Book page 40

Skills: *Reading and speaking*

Let's start! **Would you like to work in a zoo?**

12 CD1 56 **Read and listen. Then match.**

a

b

c

¹ *Meet the squirrel monkeys!*
Squirrel monkeys come from South America. They are small with grey and orange fur. They've got long tails. Squirrel monkeys like fruit, leaves, seeds and insects. They also eat flowers, eggs and small animals. They are good at climbing trees and they are very quick.

² *Meet the wallabies!*
A wallaby looks like a kangaroo but it's smaller. Wallabies come from Australia. They eat grass and plants. Wallabies can't run but they are very good at jumping.

³ *Meet our baby red panda!*
This is Bo. He's our baby red panda! Red pandas come from Asia. They are red and brown and they've got long tails. Red pandas eat lots of things. They like plants, insects, eggs, birds or small animals!

13 **Read again and answer the questions.**

1 Can squirrel monkeys climb trees?
2 What do wallabies eat?
3 Do red pandas eat meat?
4 Which animal comes from Australia?

14 About Me **Ask and answer with a friend.**

What's your favourite wild animal?
What does it look like?
Where does it come from?
What does it eat?

Writing

→ Activity Book page 41: Write about your favourite animal.

CD1 57 **Read and listen.**

Week 4
We need owl boxes

2

Are there bird boxes in your garden, Tom?

Yes, there are. But there aren't many.

3

No, Anna. We need bigger boxes. Owls are bigger than other birds.

Are these owl boxes?

Let's make one.

4

Grandpa, can you make an owl box for us?

Yes – you can help.

5

Where are the nails?

Here they are.

Can you pass them, please?

6

There you are! A house for an owl!

It's beautiful.

7

Thank you. It's for the nature zone.

Wow! There are lots of boxes.

It's an owl town!

16 CD1 58 (Talk Time) **Listen and repeat. Then act.**

kite   rubber   glue   balls   colouring pencils   scissors

1 Where's the glue?
It's here.
Can you pass it, please?
Yes, of course.

2 Where are the scissors?
They're here.
Can you pass them, please?
Yes, of course.

Say it!

17 CD1 59 **Listen and repeat.**

Frogs catch fruit flies with their tongues.

What animal group is it?

1 (CD1 60) **Listen and repeat.**

1 mammals

2 reptiles

3 amphibians

2 **Watch the video.**

3 **What animal group is it? Read and match.**

1 It's an amphibian. It can live on land and in water.
2 It's a bird and it can fly.
3 It's a fish and it can swim.
4 It's a mammal. It's got spots on it and it can climb.
5 It's a reptile and it can walk and swim.

Guess What!

The hummingbird is the only bird that can fly backwards.

1

2

3

4 **5**

4 **What group of animals would you like to film?**

Project

5 Make a mind map with the five animal groups.

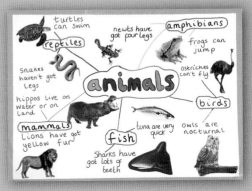

CLIL: Science **55**

Review Units 3 and 4

1 Find the words in the puzzles and match to the photos.

v*t

p*l*t

s*ng*r

*rt*st

 2 Listen and say the letters.

3 Read and answer the questions.

1 Look at picture a.
What does she do?

2 Look at picture b.
Where does she work?

3 Look at picture c.
Is the sculpture bigger or smaller than the artist?

4 Look at picture d.
Does he work on a plane?

4 Make your own word puzzles for your friend.

Choose jobs or wild animals:
k*ng*r**
g*r*ll*

→ Activity Book pages 46–47

Red
Do you want to be a (doctor)?

Blue
Does (a farmer) work in (an office)?

Yellow
Are (gorillas) (bigger) than (rabbits)?

(5) Food and drink

Guess What!

1 CD2 02 **Listen and point.**

2 CD2 03 **Listen, point and repeat.**

3 CD2 04 **Listen and answer the questions.**

4 Think **Describe and guess who.**

He wants pasta for lunch.   Tom!

1 pasta
2 yoghurt
3 soup
4 pizza
5 salad
6 nuts
7 tea
8 coffee
9 biscuit
10 crisps

5 🎧CD2 05 Listen and choose. Then sing the song.

1 I always have a sandwich/pizza for lunch,
And I usually have some fruit.
I sometimes have a yoghurt/soup,
But I never have biscuits or crisps.
No, he never has biscuits or crisps!

2 I usually have pasta/salad for dinner,
And I sometimes have some soup.
I always have some vegetables/fruit,
But I never have biscuits or crisps.
No, he never has biscuits or crisps!

He never has biscuits or crisps!

6 (Think) Look at the song. Then read and correct the sentences.

1 I never have a sandwich for lunch.
2 I always have pasta for dinner.
3 I sometimes have crisps for lunch.
4 I never have vegetables for dinner.
5 I always have biscuits for dinner.

Number 1. He always has a sandwich for lunch.

always

usually

sometimes

never

7 (About Me) Make sentences and say true or false.

I always have crisps for lunch.

False!

Remember!
I **always have** vegetables for dinner.
He **never has** biscuits for dinner.

8 (CD2 06) **Listen and repeat.**

How often do you have salad for lunch?

Every day.

Usually.

Sometimes.

Never.

9 (About Me) **Make questions. Then ask and answer with a friend.**

How often do you have

for breakfast?

for lunch?

for dinner?

10 **Tell the class about you and your friend.**

Pablo has toast for breakfast every day. I usually have yoghurt.

11 (CD2 07) **Go to page 103. Listen and repeat the chant.**

Remember!

How often do you have vegetables for lunch?
Every day. Usually. Sometimes. Never.

Skills: *Listening and speaking*

Let's start! **What do you usually have for lunch?**

12 (CD2 08) **Listen and match.**

Grace

a

Monday	Tuesday	Wednesday	Thursday
pizza	pasta	soup	sandwich
salad	vegetables	salad	salad
fruit	yoghurt	yoghurt	fruit
yoghurt	water	water	yoghurt
water			water

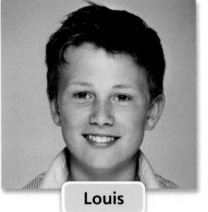

Louis

b

Monday	Tuesday	Wednesday	Thursday
sandwich	chicken	soup	pasta
salad	salad	salad	vegetables
fruit	fruit	yoghurt	fruit
yoghurt	nuts	fruit	juice
water	juice	water	

13 (CD2 08) **Listen again and answer the questions.**

1 How often does Grace have salad for lunch?
2 Does Grace sometimes have pizza?
3 How often does Louis have nuts?
4 Does Louis like yoghurt?

14 (About Me) **Ask and answer with a friend.**

Do you always have a healthy lunch?
Do you usually have fruit, vegetables or salad?
What do you never have for lunch?

Writing

→ Activity Book page 51: Make a lunch diary and write about it.

Value: Be clean around food

→ Activity Book page 52

16 CD2 10 (Talk Time) Listen and repeat. Then act.

tea   orange juice   pizza   biscuits   crisps   nuts

1

It's one pound.

How much is the orange juice?

Can I have two, please?

Yes, of course.

2

How much are the biscuits?

They're fifty pence.

Can I have three, please?

Yes, of course.

Say it!

17 CD2 11 Listen and repeat.

Aardvarks come out in the dark.

aardvark

Where does **water** come from?

1 (CD2 12) **Listen and repeat.**

1 rain

2 glacier

3 well

4 spring

2 **Watch the video.**

3 **What can you see in the pictures?**

Guess What!

About 60% of our body is made up of water.

Project

5 Make a shape poem about where water comes from.

Water falling, falling from the clouds. Rain comes down into the rivers and seas. Water, water all around from the wells and springs in the ground.

Water falling · from the clouds · into the ground · Springs and wells · Water running into · guess what the sea.

4 **Where are the big rivers in your country?**

CLIL: Science **67**

6 Health matters

Guess What!

1 Listen and point. *CD2 13*

2 Listen, point and repeat. *CD2 14*

3 Listen and answer the questions. *CD2 15*

4 *Think* Describe and guess who.

He's got a cold. Tom!

1. cold
2. cough
3. earache
4. stomachache
5. backache
6. sore throat
7. temperature
8. toothache
9. headache

5 CD2 16 Listen and match. Then sing the song.

1 Oh dear, what's the matter?
What's the matter with you, Tim?
I've got a headache.
Oh dear, poor you!

2 Oh dear, what's the matter?
What's the matter with Max?
He's got a stomachache.
Oh dear, poor him!

3 Oh dear, what's the matter?
What's the matter with Mary?
She's got a cough and a cold.
Oh dear, poor her!

a **b** **c**

6 CD2 17 Now listen and say the names.

7 Think Play a mime game.

What's the matter with Charlie?

He's got a stomachache.

Have you got a stomachache?

Yes, I have.

Remember!
What's the matter?
I've got a cough and a cold.

8 **CD2 18** **Listen and repeat.**

Can you go sailing today?

No, I can't. I've got a sore throat and a temperature.

9 **CD2 19** **Listen and match.**

10 **Think** **Ask questions and say why you can't.**

Can you go ice skating today?

No, I can't. I've got an earache.

11 **CD2 20** **Go to page 103. Listen and repeat the chant.**

Remember!

Can you play basketball today?
No, I can't. I've got a cough and a cold.

Skills: *Reading and speaking*

Let's start! How often do you have a cold?

12 (CD2 21) **Read and listen. Then match.**

Have you got a cold?

Make some lemon and honey! Lemon and honey is a very healthy drink. It's good for colds and it's easy to make! Try this simple recipe at home.

1 You need a lemon, some honey and some hot water.
2 Cut the lemon. Squeeze the juice into a cup.
3 Add some honey.
4 Add the hot water. Be careful! An adult can help.

It's ready! Now sit down and enjoy your lemon and honey!

13 **Read again and say *true* or *false*.**

1 Lemon and honey is a healthy drink.
2 It isn't good for colds.
3 It's difficult to make.
4 You need hot water for the drink.

14 (About Me) **Ask and answer with a friend.**

What healthy food or drinks can you make?
Can you make a salad?
Can you make a fruit salad?
Can you make orange juice?
Can you make a sandwich?

Writing

→ Activity Book page 59: Write a recipe for a healthy food or drink.

1 Week 6
We need skateboards.

Let's ask our cousin, Chris!

He goes to skateboarding club today.

2

3 Skateboarding competition today
Win a skateboard!

It's a competition!

Go, Chris!

4 Oh dear!

Are you OK, Chris?

Yes, I think so. My leg hurts, but I'm OK. Don't worry.

5 Have you got a headache, Chris?

No, I'm OK now.

But where's your skateboard?

6 Skateboarding competition today
Win a skateboard!

Max!

He's really good!

7 That's OK! I'm good at skateboarding, but Max is very good!

Well done, Max!

Sorry, Chris!

1

74 Value: Be a good sport

→ Activity Book page 60

16 (CD2 23) (Talk Time) **Listen and repeat. Then act.**

backache   earache   headache   temperature   sore throat   cough

1

Are you OK?

Yes, I think so. Don't worry.

Oh, good!

2

Are you OK?

No, I don't think so. I've got a headache.

Oh dear!

Say it!

17 (CD2 24) **Listen and repeat.**

Spiders spin special webs.

spider

What can we use
plants
for?

Listen and repeat.

fabric   fuel   medicine

2 Watch the video.

3 Listen and say what picture it is.

Guess What!

Some bamboo plants can grow almost one metre in a day.

Project

5 Make a poster to show what plants are used for.

medicine   fuel

What can we use plants for?

shelter

fabric   food and drink

4 Can you think of something new you could make from a plant?

→ Activity Book page 62

Review Units 5 and 6

1 Find the words and match to the photos.

pizzalpastapsaladesoup

2 CD2 27 Listen and say the names.

3 Read and say the names.

1 She likes making salad.
2 He sometimes makes pizza.
3 He likes making soup.
4 She often makes pasta with chicken and vegetables.

4 Make your own word puzzle for your friend.

Choose food or health:
toothachebcoughocold

Joe

Will

Rosie

Sara

(7) Buildings

Guess What!

CD2 28 **Listen and point.**

 **CD2 29** **Listen, point and repeat.**

3 **CD2 30** **Listen and answer the questions.**

4 **Think** **Describe and guess where.**

There are lots of old toys here.

Attic!

❶ ground floor	❻ roof		
❷ first floor	❼ basement		
❸ second floor	❽ garage		
❹ third floor	❾ stairs		
❺ lift	❿ attic		

5 (CD2 31) **Listen and choose. Then sing the song.**

1 Where were you yesterday?
Where were you yesterday morning?
I was in the kitchen/living room,
In my flat on the second floor.

2 Where were you yesterday?
Where were you yesterday afternoon?
I was in the living room/bedroom,
In my flat on the second floor.

3 Where were you yesterday?
Where were you yesterday evening?
I was in the roof garden/attic,
Above my flat on the second floor.
My flat on the second floor.
The second floor. The second floor.

6 (CD2 32) **Listen and say the names.**

John   Marta   Leon   Lola

7 (About Me) **Ask and answer with a friend.**

Where were you yesterday morning?

I was at home. I was in the living room.

Remember!
Where were you yesterday morning?
I was in the kitchen.

8 CD2 33 **Listen and repeat.**

Were you at home last night?

No, I wasn't. I was at the cinema.

Yes, I was.

Were you at home?

9 Think **Make questions. Ask and answer with a friend.**

Questions

Were you

at home
at school
at the cinema
at a restaurant
on the bus
in hospital
at a shopping centre
at the swimming pool

yesterday morning?
yesterday afternoon?
yesterday evening?
last night?

10 About Me **Play a guessing game.**

Were you in hospital last night?

No, I wasn't. Guess again.

11 CD2 34 **Go to page 103. Listen and repeat the chant.**

Remember!

Were you at home last night?
Yes, I was.   No, I wasn't.

Skills: *Listening and speaking*

Let's start! **Who's your favourite singer?**

12 (CD2 35) **Look at Misha's diary. Listen and choose.**

Misha

Saturday

Morning
at home / in a hotel / at a shopping centre

Lunch
in a restaurant / at home / in a park

Afternoon
at home / in the recording studio / at the cinema

Evening
in a hotel / at home / at a concert

13 (CD2 35) **Listen again and answer the questions.**

1   Where was Misha in the morning?
2   Where was she at lunch?
3   Where was she in the afternoon?
4   Where was she in the evening?

14 (About Me) **Ask and answer with a friend.**

Where were you on Saturday morning?
Where were you on Sunday afternoon?
Were you at the park on Saturday?
Were you at a concert on Saturday evening?

Writing

→ Activity Book page 69: Choose one day. Where were you? Write a diary for that day.

16 CD2 37 (Talk Time) **Listen and repeat. Then act.**

grandpa   Ben   Jane   grandma   Lara   Uncle John

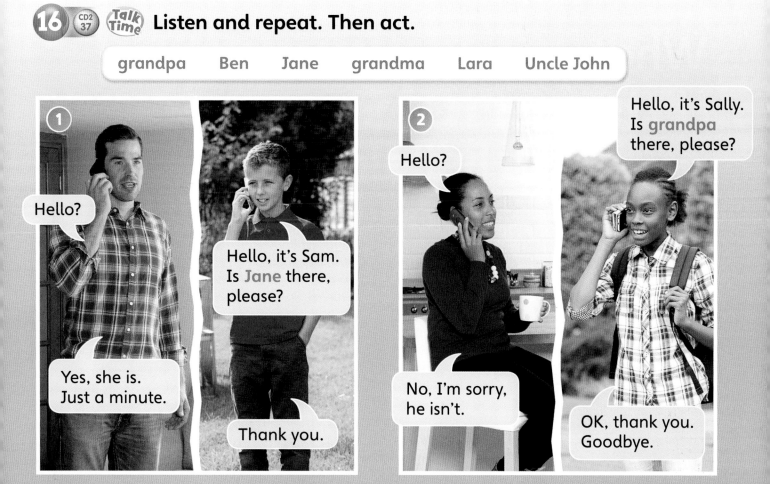

1

Hello?

Hello, it's Sam. Is Jane there, please?

Yes, she is. Just a minute.

Thank you.

2

Hello?

Hello, it's Sally. Is grandpa there, please?

No, I'm sorry, he isn't.

OK, thank you. Goodbye.

Say it!

17 CD2 38 **Listen and repeat.**

Black ducks stand on rocks.

black duck

What materials were buildings made of?

1 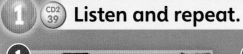 **Listen and repeat.**

1
clay

2
stone

3
animal skins

2 **Watch the video.**

3 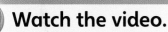 **What are these buildings made of?**

1

2

3

4

4 **What different things are made of stone?**

Guess What!

Animal skins were used for water bottles in the eighth century.

Project

5 Make a fact file about an old building in your country.

Building: castle
Country: Spain
Material: stone

This is Santa Catalina Castle. It's got lots of windows but they're very small. In this beautiful castle there's a hotel and a swimming pool!

8 Weather

Guess What!

1 (CD2 40) Listen and point.

2 (CD2 41) Listen, point and repeat.

Today's weather

Temperature **1**

3

Weather **2**

4

5

6

7

8

9

1 hot
2 sunny
3 cold
4 warm
5 snowy
6 cloudy
7 foggy
8 windy
9 rainy

3 (CD2 42) Listen and say the numbers.

4 (About Me) Ask and answer with a friend.

Do you like cold weather?   No, I don't. I like hot weather.

5 CD2 43 **Listen and match. Then sing the song.**

1 What was the weather like yesterday?
It was cold and rainy.
What's the weather like today?
It's hot and sunny.
Today it's hot and sunny.
So we can go out and play.
Hooray!

2 What was the weather like yesterday?
It was cold and foggy.
What's the weather like today?
It's cold and snowy.
Today it's cold and snowy.
So we can go out and play.
Hooray!

6 CD2 44 **Listen and answer the questions.**

yesterday morning

yesterday afternoon

yesterday evening

last night

7 Think **Ask and answer with a friend. Say true or false.**

What was the weather like yesterday?

It was cold and snowy.

False! It was cold and rainy.

Remember!
It was cold and rainy yesterday.
It's hot and sunny today.

→ Activity Book page 75

8 (CD2 45) **Listen and repeat.**

1 Was it cloudy on Monday?

No, it wasn't. It was hot and sunny.

2 Was it rainy on Saturday?

Yes, it was.

9 (CD2 46) **Look at the weather diary. Listen and answer the questions.**

Weather diary

Mon	Tues	Wed	Thurs	Fri	Sat	Sun

10 (About Me) **Make a weather diary. Ask and answer with a friend.**

Was it hot and sunny on Saturday?

No, it wasn't. It was cold and rainy.

11 (CD2 47) **Go to page 103. Listen and repeat the chant.**

Remember!

Was it hot and sunny on Monday?
Yes, it was.   No, it wasn't.

Skills: *Reading and speaking*

Let's start! **Is it snowy in your country?**

12 CD2 48 **Read and listen. Then match.**

○ ○ ○ ◀ ▶

Hi Kalu,

[1] How are you? I'm fine. It was my birthday on Saturday. I'm eleven now. My birthday was great. It was a cold and snowy day and I was at the Sapporo Snow Festival with my family.

[2] The snow festival is every year in February. It's fantastic. It's really big and there are lots of amazing snow sculptures. This is a photo of my favourite snow sculpture this year. Can you see what it is? It's a snow building.

[3] There are also snow animals and lots of snowmen and women. This is a snow family!

[4] The snow festival is beautiful at night too. What's your favourite festival?

Email me soon.

Best wishes,

Yasuko

13 **Read and say *true* or *false*.**

1 Yasuko's birthday was on Sunday.
2 Yasuko was at the snow festival with her friends.
3 The snow festival is every April.
4 Yasuko likes the snow festival.
5 You can see lots of snow sculptures at the festival.

14 **About Me** **Ask and answer with a friend.**

When's your birthday? What festivals do you have in your country? What's your favourite festival?

Writing

→ Activity Book page 77: Write about your favourite festival.

16 CD2 50 (Talk Time) **Listen and repeat. Then act.**

TV programme   talent show   film   snow festival
birthday party   swimming competition

1
When does the film start?

At five o'clock.

Hurry up! We're late.

2
What time does the birthday party start?

OK, we have time.

At half past seven.

Say it!

17 CD2 51 **Listen and repeat.**

Elands eat grass and are land animals.

eland

→ Activity Book page 79   Function: Asking when things start   Pronunciation: *nd*   **97**

What's the **weather** like around the **world?**

1 (CD2 52) Listen and repeat.

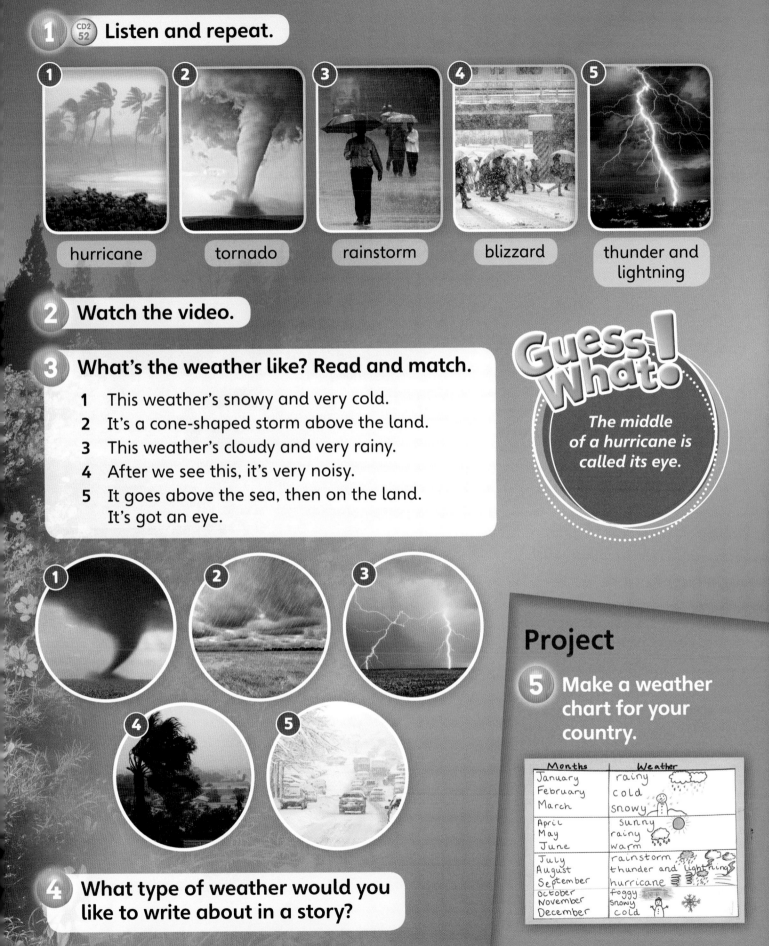

1 hurricane

2 tornado

3 rainstorm

4 blizzard

5 thunder and lightning

2 Watch the video.

3 What's the weather like? Read and match.

1 This weather's snowy and very cold.
2 It's a cone-shaped storm above the land.
3 This weather's cloudy and very rainy.
4 After we see this, it's very noisy.
5 It goes above the sea, then on the land. It's got an eye.

Guess What!

The middle of a hurricane is called its eye.

Project

5 Make a weather chart for your country.

Months	Weather	
January	rainy	
February	cold	
March	snowy	
April	sunny	
May	rainy	
June	warm	
July	rainstorm	
August	thunder and lightning	
September	hurricane	
October	foggy	
November	snowy	
December	cold	

4 What type of weather would you like to write about in a story?

→ Activity Book page 80

CLIL: Geography **99**

Review Units 7 and 8

1 **Find the words and match to the photos.**

ysown

nusny

yiran

dinwy

2 **CD2 53** **Listen and say the letters.**

3 **Read and answer.**

1 Look at picture a. What was the weather like?

2 Look at picture b. Was it sunny?

3 Look at picture c. Where was she?

4 Look at picture d. Was he at the beach?

4 **Make your own word puzzles for your friend.**

Choose weather or places in a building: orof tiasrs mbtaense

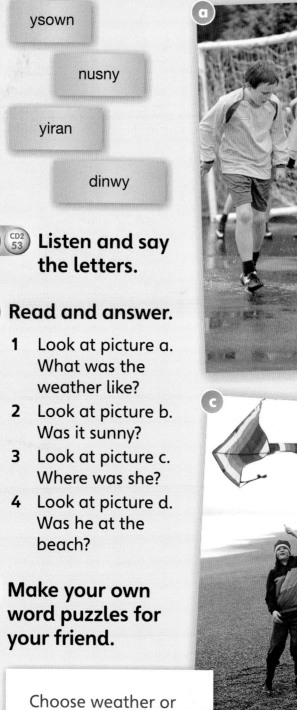

5 Play the game.

Yesterday at half past twelve …

Mrs Long

Lucy

Mr Long

Miles

Player 1
1 Was it windy?
2 Was it hot?
3 Where was the cat?
4 Where was the gorilla?
5 Was the bike in the garage?
6 Was Lucy in the attic?

Player 2
1 Was it snowy?
2 Was it cold?
3 Where was the dog?
4 Where was the penguin?
5 Was the parrot in the kitchen?
6 Was Miles in the basement?

Chants

Welcome back! (page 8)

 Listen and repeat the chant.

Ten, twenty, thirty,
Forty, fifty, sixty,
Seventy, eighty, ninety
And one hundred!
I can count to one hundred.

Ten, twenty, thirty,
Forty, fifty, sixty,
Seventy, eighty, ninety
And one hundred!
I can count to one hundred.

Unit 1 (page 18)

 Listen and repeat the chant.

Are you good at skiing?
Yes, I am. Yes, I am.
What are you good at?
I'm good at skiing.

Are you good at ice skating?
No, I'm not. No, I'm not.
What are you good at?
I'm good at roller skating.

Unit 2 (page 28)

 Listen and repeat the chant.

Start at the traffic lights!
Go straight ahead.
Turn left at the bank.
Stop! Stop! Stop!

Start at the traffic lights!
Go straight ahead.
Turn right at the park.
Stop! Stop! Stop!

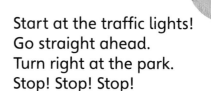

Unit 3 (page 40)

 Listen and repeat the chant.

What do you want to be?
I want to be a singer.
Do you want to be a singer?
Yes, I do. Yes, I do.

Do you want to be a teacher?
No, I don't. No, I don't.
I want to be a doctor.
George wants to be a doctor.

Unit 4 (page 50)

 Listen and repeat the chant.

Are giraffes taller than penguins?
Yes, they are. Yes, they are.
Are koalas noisier than bears?
No, they aren't. No, they aren't.

Are snakes longer than crocodiles?
Yes, they are. Yes, they are.
Are frogs bigger than owls?
No, they aren't. No, they aren't.

Unit 5 (page 62)

11 **Listen and repeat the chant.**

How often do you have salad for lunch?
Every day. Every day.
I have salad for lunch every day.
He has salad for lunch every day.

How often do you have toast for breakfast?
Never. Never. Never.
I never have toast for breakfast.
She never has toast for breakfast.

Unit 6 (page 72)

11 **Listen and repeat the chant.**

Can you go sailing today?
No, I can't. No, I can't.
I've got a sore throat and a temperature.
Oh dear! A sore throat and a temperature.

Can you play basketball today?
No, I can't. No, I can't.
I've got a cough and a cold.
Oh dear! A cough and a cold.

Unit 7 (page 84)

11 **Listen and repeat the chant.**

Were you at home last night?
Yes, I was. Yes, I was.
I was at home.

Were you at home last night?
No, I wasn't. No, I wasn't.
I was at the cinema.

Unit 8 (page 94)

11 **Listen and repeat the chant.**

Was it hot and sunny on Monday?
Yes, it was. Yes, it was.
It was hot and sunny.

Was it hot and sunny on Tuesday?
No, it wasn't. No, it wasn't.
It was cloudy.

Thanks and Acknowledgements

Many thanks to everyone in the excellent team at Cambridge University Press. In particular we would like to thank Emily Hird, Liane Grainger and Camilla Agnew whose professionalism, enthusiasm, experience and talent makes them all such a pleasure to work with.

We would also like to give special thanks to Lesley Koustaff for her unfailing support, expert guidance, good humour and welcome encouragement throughout the project.

The authors and publishers would like to thank the following contributors:

Blooberry Design: concept design, cover design, book design, page make-up
Christine Barton: editing
Ann Thomson: art direction, picture research
Gareth Boden: commissioned photography
Ian Harker: audio recording
Robert Lee, Dib Dib Dub Studios: song and chant composition
Vince Cross: theme tune composition
James Richardson: arrangement of theme tune
Phaebus: video production

The authors and publishers acknowledge the following sources of copyright material and are grateful for the permissions granted. While every effort has been made, it has not always been possible to identify the sources of all the material used, or to trace all copyright holders.

If any omissions are brought to our notice, we will be happy to include the appropriate acknowledgements on reprinting.

The authors and publishers would like to thank the following illustrators:

Pablo Gallego (Beehive Illustration) 5, 6, 10, 15, 16, 25, 26, 30, 37, 38, 42, 47, 48, 52, 59, 60, 64, 69, 70, 74, 81, 82, 86, 91, 92, 96; Luke Newell 7, 17, 27, 39, 49, 61, 71, 83, 93; A Corazon Abierto (Sylvie Poggio Artists) 18, 28, 40, 94; Marcus Cutler (Sylvie Poggio Artists) 35, 57, 79, 101

The authors and publishers would like to thank the following for permission to reproduce photographs:

p.2–3: Tatiana Popova/Shutterstock; p.4–5: Yi Lu/Viewstock/Corbis; p.8 (1), p.8 (2): Johnny Greig/Getty Images; p.8 (3): OJO Images Ltd/Alamy; p.8 (4): Bejim/Shutterstock; p.8 (5): Sergey Pavlov/Getty Images; p.9 (B/G): Iakov Kalinin/Shutterstock; p.9 (a): Kuttig – People/Alamy; p.9 (b): Datacraft – Sozaijiten/Alamy; p.9 (c), p.50 (3): Juniors Bildarchiv GmbH/Alamy; p.11 (B/G), p.87 (B/G): Robert Harding Picture Library Ltd/Alamy; p.11 (BR): All Canada Photos/Alamy; p.12–13: Thierry GRUN/Alamy; p.13 (T-1): Daniela Pelazza/Shutterstock; p.13 (T-2): Jani Bryson/Getty Images; p.13 (T-3): Philippe Intraligi/Ikon Images/Corbis; p.13 (T-4): MT511/Shutterstock; p.13 (CL): irin-k/Shutterstock; p.13 (CR): Moiz Husein Dossaji/Shutterstock; p.13 (BL): Photoshot Holdings Ltd/Alamy; p.13 (BC): Jiri Vaclavek/Shutterstock; p.14–15: mediacolor's/Alamy; p.17 (B): Pakhnyushchy/Shutterstock; p.19 (B/G): Lora liu/Shutterstock; p.19 (TL): Sean Justice/Shutterstock; p.19 (TC): Nikoncharly/Getty Images; p.19 (TR): Digital Vision/Getty Images; p.21 (B/G), p.65 (B/G), p.97 (B/G): David Cayless/Getty Images; p.21 (BR): SuperStock/Alamy; p.22: Mira/Alamy; p.23 (T-1): I love images/Getty Images; p.23 (T-2): Thomas Perkins/Getty Images; p.23 (T-3): Image Source Plus/Alamy; p.23 (T-4): J and J Productions/Getty Images; p.23 (T-5): Chris Stein/Getty Images; p.23 (CL): Radius Images/Alamy; p.23 (C): Amy Myers/Shutterstock; p.23 (BL): @Michi B./Getty Images; p.23 (BC): F1online digitale Bildagentur GmbH/Alamy; p.24–25: Andrey Pronin/ZUMA Press/Corbis; p.29 (B/G): QQ7/Shutterstock; p.29 (T): Greg Williams/REX; p.29 (C): tim gartside london/Alamy; p.29 (BL): Imagestate Media Partners Limited – Impact Photos/Alamy; (BR): Michael Kemp/Alamy; p.31 (B/G), p.43 (B/G): Barry Downard/Getty Images; p.31 (BR): Mauricio Handler/Getty Images; p.32: Zoonar GmbH/Alamy; p.33 (T-1): Dan Kosmayer/Shutterstock; p.33 (T-2): Laborant/Shutterstock; p.33 (T-3): GeorgeMPhotography/Shutterstock; p.33 (T-4): poparstic/Shutterstock; p.33 (T-5): KULISH VIKTORIIA/Shutterstock; p.33 (CL): American Spirit/Shutterstock; p.33 (C): View Pictures/Getty Images; p.33 (CR): Elnur/Shutterstock; p.33 (BL): Sergio Bertino/Shutterstock; p.33 (BC): Styve Reineck/Shutterstock; p.34 (TL): Denis Radovanovic/Shutterstock; p.34 (TR): Michael DeYoung/Blend Images/Corbis; p.34 (BL): Pictorium/Alamy; p.34 (BR): tab62/Shutterstock; p.36–37: Simon GRATIEN/Getty Images; p.39 (a), p.41 (BC), p.84 (CR): Monkey Business Images/Shutterstock; p.39 (b): StockLite/Shutterstock; p.39 (c): Juice Images/Alamy; p.39 (d): Horizons WWP/Alamy; p.41 (B/G): fototrav/Getty Images; p.41 (TL): v.s.anandhakrishna/Shutterstock; p.41 (TC): Byelikova Oksana/Shutterstock; p.41 (TR): Lumi images/Alamy; p.41 (BL): holbox/Shutterstock; p.41 (BR): Klaus Vedfelt/Getty Images; p.43 (BR): Rainer von Brandis/Getty Images; p.44: Tom Bean/Alamy; p.45 (T-1): Grzegorz Petrykowski/Shutterstock; p.45 (T-2): Leandro Mise/Alamy; p.45 (T-3): Lloyd Sutton/Alamy; p.45 (T-4): RosalreneBetancourt5/Alamy; p.45 (CL): David R. Frazier Photolibrary, Inc./Alamy; p.45 (CR): Nature Picture Library/Alamy; p.45 (BL): ITAR-TASS Photo Agency/Alamy; p.45 (BC): Steve Arnold/Alamy; p.46–47: Thomas Marent/Minden Pictures/Corbis; p.50 (1): Dirk Ercken/Shutterstock; p.50 (2): Milosz_M/Shutterstock; p.50 (4): Jl de Wet/Shutterstock; p.50 (BL): Ryan M. Bolton/Shutterstock; p.50 (BC-penguin): Anton_Ivanov/Shutterstock; p.50 (BC-rabbit): Andrew Parkinson/Corbis; p.50 (BR): Louise Murray/Robert Harding World Imagery/Corbis; p.51 (B/G): Subbotina Anna/Shutterstock; p.51 (B/G-inset); p.51 (TL): Oli Scarff/Getty Images; p.51 (a): Miso Lisanin/Xinhua Press/Corbis; p.51 (b): Gerry Pearce/Alamy; p.51 (c): frans lemmens/Alamy; p.53 (B/G), p.75 (B/G): SZE FEI WONG/Getty Images; p.53 (BR): Cathy Keifer/Shutterstock; p.54: Thomas Dressier/Getty Images; p.55 (1-TL): Ricardo Canino/Shutterstock; p.55 (1-TR): Johan Swanepoel/Shutterstock; p.55 (2-TL): subin pumsom/Shutterstock; p.55 (2-TR); p.55 (3-TL): Matt Jeppson/Shutterstock; p.55 (3-TR): reptiles4all/Shutterstock; p.55 (CL): Bill Kennedy/Shutterstock; p.55 (C): Dirk Ercken/Shutterstock; p.55 (CR): Audrey Snider-Bell/Shutterstock; p.55 (BL): Mikadun/Shutterstock; p.55 (BC): Jean-Edouard Rozey/Shutterstock; p.56 (TL): C Flanigan/FilmMagic/Getty Images; p.56 (TR): Hugo Ortuno Suarez/Getty Images; p.56 (BL): Stock Connection Blue/Alamy; p.56 (BR), p.89 (BR): Hemis/Alamy; p.58–59: Richard Rudisill/Getty Images; p.62 (salad): Nitr/Shutterstock; p.62 (toast): triocean/Shutterstock; p.62 (burger): page frederique/Shutterstock; p.62 (ice cream): M. Unal Ozmen/Shutterstock; p.62 (fruit): Lestertair/Shutterstock; p.62 (veg), p.77 (BL): Africa Studio/Shutterstock; p.62 (sandwich): Food and Drink Photos/Alamy; p.62 (chicken): papkin/Shutterstock; p.62 (pasta): marmo81/Shutterstock; p.62 (fish): TAGSTOCK1/Shutterstock; p.62 (nuts): Suprun Vitaly/Shutterstock; p.62 (yoghurt): nito/Shutterstock; p.63 (B/G): Marina Grau/Shutterstock; p.63 (TL): TS/Alamy; p.63 (CL): sanneberg/Shutterstock; p.63 (BR): David Papazian/Corbis; p.65 (BR): Nigel J. Dennis/Corbis; p.66: Paul Souders/Corbis; p.67 (T-1): sondem/Shutterstock; p.67 (T-2): Lex van Groningen/Buiten-beeld/Minden Pictures/Corbis; p.67 (T-3): Art Directors & TRIP/Alamy; p.67 (T-4): Denis Kichatof/Shutterstock; p.67 (CL): peresanz/Shutterstock; p.67 (CR), p.93 (BC-afternoon): imageBROKER/Alamy; p.67 (BC): Julian Love/JAI/Corbis; p.67 (BC): Dori Moreno/Getty Images; p.68–69: Hero Images/Getty Images; p.72 (1): Fabrice LEROUGE/Getty Images; p.72 (3): Bob Mitchell/Corbis; p.72 (a): Agencja Fotograficzna Caro/Alamy; p.72 (b): Michael Krasowitz/Getty Images; p.72 (c): Radius Images/Alamy; p.72 (d): BSIP SA/Alamy; p.73 (B/G): Irina Mos/Shutterstock; p.73 (B/G-inset): Malivan_Iuliia/Shutterstock; p.73 (BL): Klaus Vedfelt/Getty Images; p.75 (BR): Chris Cheadle/Alamy; p.76: Everything/Shutterstock; p.77 (1-TL): Destinyweddingstudio/Shutterstock; p.77 (1-TR): Mikhail Pozhenko/Shutterstock; p.77 (2-TL): Denis Tabler/Shutterstock; p.77 (2-TR): tristan tan/Shutterstock; p.77 (3-TL), p.83 (Lola): Gallo Images/Alamy; p.77 (3-TR): Antonova Anna/Shutterstock; p.77 (CL): John Elk III/Getty Images; p.77 (C): Elly Godfroy/Alamy; p.77 (CR): Alexandr Makarov/Shutterstock; p.77 (BC): my nordic/Shutterstock; p.78 (TL): Brachat, Oliver/the4 food passionates/Corbis; p.78 (TR): 2/Andersen Ross/Ocean/Corbis; p.78 (BL): Bloomimage/Corbis; p.78 (BR): Food Centrale Hamburg GmbH/Alamy; p.80–81: Krzysztof Dydynski/Getty Images; p.83 (John): Jupiterimages/Getty Images; p.83 (Marta): kali9/Getty Images; p.83 (Leon): David Burton/Alamy; p.84 (CL): Khakimullin Aleksandr/Shutterstock; p.84 (B): Christian Mueller/Shutterstock; p.85 (B/G): balabolka/Shutterstock; p.85 (TL): Andre Babiak/Alamy; p.85 (BL): dwphotos/Shutterstock; p.87 (BR): KathyKafka/Getty Images; p.88: Sasa Komien/Shutterstock; p.89 (TC): Pecold/Shutterstock; p.89 (TR): ARCTIC IMAGES/Alamy; p.89 (CL): saras66/Shutterstock; p.89 (CR): kosmos111/Shutterstock; p.89 (BL): Evgeny Prokofyev/Getty Images; p.89 (BC): David South/Alamy; p.89 (BR-inset): Noradoa/Shutterstock; p.90–91: All Canada Photos/Alamy; p.93 (BL): shotstock/Alamy; p.93 (BC-evening); p.93 (BR): Cal Vornberger/Alamy; p.95 (B/G): nodff/Shutterstock; p.95 (a): JTB MEDIA CREATION, Inc/Alamy; p.95 (b): stock_shot/Shutterstock; p.95 (c): Ulana Switucha/Alamy; p.95 (d): wisarut_ch/Shutterstock; p.97 (BR): MIKEL BILBAO GOROSTIAGA-NATURE & LANDSCAPES/Alamy; p.98: Wan Ru Chen/Getty Images; p.99 (T-1): Mike Hill/Alamy; p.99 (T-2): Cultura Science/Jason Persoff Stormdoctor/ Getty Images; p.99 (T-3): epa european pressphoto agency b.v./Alamy; p.99 (T-4): Petri Artturi Asikinen/Getty Images; p.99 (T-5): Australian Land, City, People Scape Photographer/Getty Images; p.99 (CL): Aaron Horowitz/Corbis; p.99 (C): peresanz/Shutterstock; p.99 (CR): Jim Reed/Jim Reed Photography – Severe&/Corbis; p.99 (BL): Gregory Pelt/Shutterstock; p.99 (BC): Igumnova Irina/Shutterstock; p.100 (TL): Adrian Sherratt/Alamy; p.100 (TR): Golden Pixels LLC/Alamy; p.100 (BL): Stockbyte/Getty Images; p.100 (BR): benedektibor/Getty Images; p.102 (B/G), p.103 (B/G): blue67design/Shutterstock; p.102 (T), p.102 (C), p.102 (BL), p.102 (BR), p.103 (T), p.103 (CR), p.103 (BL), p.103 (BC), p.103 (BR): Elena Schweitzer/Shutterstock.

Commissioned photography by Gareth Boden: p.11 (T); p.13 (BR); p.18 (T); p.21 (T); p.23 (BR); p.31 (T); p.33 (BR); p.40 (T); p.43 (T); p.45 (T); p.50 (T); p.53 (T); p.55 (BR); p.62 (T); p.65 (T); p.67 (BR); p.71 (B); p.72 (T); p.72 (2); p.72 (4); p.73 (a–d); p.75 (T); p.77 (BR); p.84 (T); p.87 (T); p.89 (BR); p.94 (T); p.97 (T); p.99 (BR)

Our special thanks to the following for their kind help during location photography:

Queen Emma Primary School

Front Cover photo by Gerardo Ricardo Lopez/Getty Images